AL•LEONARD

STRUMENTAL
PLAY-ALONG

AUDIO
ACCESS
INCLUDED

LAYBACK+
ed • Pitch • Balance • Loop

FLUTE

HIP-HOP HITS

Audio arrangements by Peter Deneff

To access audio, visit:
www.halleonard.com/mylibrary

Enter Code
1622-2096-0048-8115

ISBN 978-1-5400-8258-9

Visit Hal Leonard Online at
www.halleonard.com

Contact us:
Hal Leonard
7777 West Bluemound Road
Milwaukee, WI 53213
Email: info@halleonard.com

In Europe, contact:
Hal Leonard Europe Limited
42 Wigmore Street
Marylebone, London, W1U 2RN
Email: info@halleonardeurope.com

In Australia, contact:
Hal Leonard Australia Pty. Ltd.
4 Lentara Court
Cheltenham, Victoria, 3192 Australia
Email: info@halleonard.com.au

CONTENTS

4   **Bang Bang (Rap Version)**

6   **Goodbyes**

8   **Hold Up**

10   **Juice**

12   **Let You Down**

14   **Lucid Dreams**

16   **Old Town Road (Remix)**

18   **Sucker for Pain**

20   **Sunflower**

5   **Talk**

24   **Truth Hurts**

22   **Work**

BANG BANG
(Rap Version)

FLUTE

Words and Music by ONIKA MARAJ,
MAX MARTIN, SAVAN KOTECHA
and RICKARD GÖRANSSON

TALK

FLUTE

Words and Music by KHALID ROBINSON,
GUY LAWRENCE and HOWARD LAWRENCE

GOODBYES

Flute

Words and Music by AUSTIN POST,
BRIAN LEE, LOUIS BELL,
WILLIAM WALSH, JEFFREY LAMAR WILLIAMS,
VAL BLAVATNIK and JESSIE LAUREN FOUTZ

HOLD UP

Flute

Words and Music by BEYONCÉ KNOWLES,
UZOECHI EMENIKE, DEANDRE WAY, DOC POMUS,
MORT SHUMAN, SEAN RHODEN, KAREN ORZOLEK,
NICHOLAS ZINNER, BRIAN CHASE, KELVIN McCONNELL,
ANTONIO RANDOLPH, EMILE HAYNIE, THOMAS PENTZ,
JOSHUA TILLMAN and EZRA KOENIG

JUICE

Flute

Words and Music by LIZZO,
THERON MAKIEL THOMAS, ERIC FREDERIC,
SAM SUMSER and SEAN SMALL

To Coda

D.S. al Coda

CODA

LET YOU DOWN

FLUTE

Words and Music by TOMMEE PROFITT
and NATE FEUERSTEIN

LUCID DREAMS

Flute

Words and Music by JARAD HIGGINS,
DOMINIC MILLER, GORDON SUMNER,
DANNY SNODGRASS JR. and NICHOLAS MIRA

mf

OLD TOWN ROAD
(Remix)

Flute

Words and Music by TRENT REZNOR,
BILLY RAY CYRUS, JOCELYN DONALD,
ATTICUS ROSS, KIOWA ROUKEMA
and MONTERO LAMAR HILL

SUCKER FOR PAIN

Flute

Words and Music by ALEX GRANT, WAYNE SERMON,
DANIEL REYNOLDS, BENJAMIN McKEE, DANIEL PLATZMAN,
DWAYNE CARTER, ROBERT HALL, CAMERON THOMAZ,
TYRONE WILLIAMS GRIFFIN JR. and SAM HARRIS

To Coda ⊕

D.S. al Coda

CODA ⊕

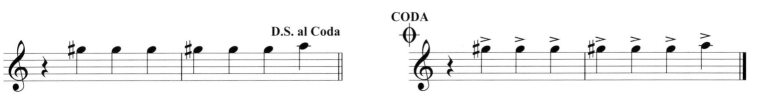

SUNFLOWER

from SPIDER-MAN: INTO THE SPIDER-VERSE

Flute

Words and Music by AUSTIN RICHARD POST,
CARL AUSTIN ROSEN, KHALIF BROWN,
CARTER LANG, LOUIS BELL
and BILLY WALSH

WORK

Words and Music by ROBYN FENTY,
JAHRON BRATHWAITE, ALLEN RITTER,
AUBREY GRAHAM, MATTHEW SAMUELS,
MONTE S. MOIR and RICHARD STEPHENSON

Flute

To Coda ⊕

CODA ⊕

D.S. al Coda

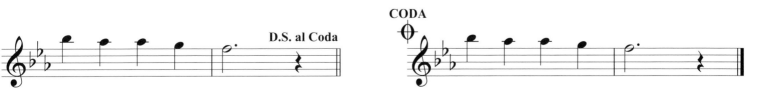

TRUTH HURTS

FLUTE

Words and Music by LIZZO,
ERIC FREDERIC, JESSE ST. JOHN GELLER
and STEVEN CHEUNG